C000102842

methuen | drama

LONDON · NEW YORK · OXFORD · NEW DELHI · SYDNEY

METHUEN DRAMA
Bloomsbury Publishing Plc
50 Bedford Square, London, WC1B 3DP, UK
1385 Broadway, New York, NY 10018, USA
29 Earlsfort Terrace, Dublin 2, Ireland

BLOOMSBURY, METHUEN DRAMA and the Methuen
Drama logo are trademarks of Bloomsbury Publishing Plc

First published in Great Britain 2021

A catalogue record for this book is available from the British Library.

A catalog record for this book is available from the Library of Congress.

ISBN: PB: 978-1-3502-8042-7
ePDF: 978-1-3502-8043-4
eBook: 978-1-3502-8044-1

Series: Modern Plays

Typeset by Mark Heslington Ltd, Scarborough, North Yorkshire
Printed and bound in Great Britain

To find out more about our authors and books visit
www.bloomsbury.com and sign up for our newsletters.

CAST

Roger	Mark Lambert
Erin	Lisa Zahra
Isla/PC Jones	Catrin Aaron

CREATIVE

Writer	Tim Price
Director	Tamara Harvey
Designer	Camilla Clarke
Lighting Designer	Ryan Joseph Stafford
Sound Designer	Beth Duke
Assistant Director	Francesca Goodridge
Assistant Director	Liv Stenström
Line Producer	Nick Stevenson
Production Manager	Jim Davis
Costume Supervisor	Debbie Knight
Special Effects	Antony Walters
Company Stage Manager	Andrew Holton
Deputy Stage Manager	Caitlin Shay
Casting Director	Amy Ball

CAST

Mark Lambert (Roger)

Mark was nominated for an Olivier Award for *Juno and the Paycock* (Albery). Recent theatre credits include *The Ferryman* (Gielgud and Broadway) and *The Phlebotomist* (Hampstead). Other theatre credits include: *All's Well That Ends Well* (Royal Shakespeare Company and Gielgud), *The Memory of Water* (Vaudeville), *Our Country's Good* (Royal Court), *Dancing at Lughnasa* (Phoenix), *Long Day's Journey into Night* (Young Vic) and *The Gigli Concert* (Abbey and Druid). TV and film include: *Cracker*, *Vanity Fair*, *Sharpe's Regiment*, *Frost*, *Bottom*, *The Young Ones*, *Veronica Guerin*, *Evelyn* and recently *Agatha and the Curse of Ishtar* and *Red Election*.

Lisa Zahra (Erin)

Lisa has previously performed at Theatr Clwyd in *The Voyage* in 2008. Theatre credits include: *The Children of Glyndwr* (ETT), *Macbeth* (Royal National Theatre), *Mission Control / Before I Leave* (National Theatre Wales), *The Kite Runner* (West End / Dubai Opera), *A Thousand Splendid Suns* (Birmingham Rep/Northern Stage/Hackney Empire), *Out of the Dark* (Rose Theatre), *Romeo and Juliet* (CUNARD), *Cymbeline* and *The Merchant of Venice* (WTC). TV/film include: *Golden Apple* (BBC), *Requiem* (Netflix), *Skellig* (Sky Movies), *Torchwood* (BBC) and *Assassin's Creed*. Lisa can be heard regularly on BBC Radio 4, where she was the voice of Malala Yousafzai in *We Are Displaced* and is currently playing Yara in the series *The Learners*.

Catrin Aaron (Isla/PC Jones)

Catrin is an Associate for Theatr Clwyd where her work includes *Missing Julie*, *Orpheus Descending*, *The Rise and Fall of Little Voice*, *Cat on a Hot Tin Roof* and *All My Sons* amongst many more. Other recent theatre work includes: *The Lovely Bones* (Birmingham Rep), *Macbeth*, *As You Like*, *Hamlet* (Shakespeare's Globe), *The Wizard of Oz* (Sheffield Crucible), *Henry V* (Regent's Park Open Air Theatre) and *Sex and the Three Day Week* (Liverpool Playhouse). Television and film includes: *Carnival Row* (Amazon Prime), *The Indian Doctor* (BBC), *The Bastard Executioner* (FX) and *Apostle* (Netflix).

CREATIVE

Writer (Tim Price)

Tim's plays include: *For Once*, *Salt Root and Roe* (winner of Best English Language playwright at the Theatre Critics of Wales Award), *Demos*, *The Radicalisation of Bradley Manning* (winner of the James Tait Black Prize for Drama), *I'm with the Band*, *Protest Song*, *Praxis Makes Perfect*, *The Insatiable, Inflatable Candylion* and *Teh Internet Is Serious Business*. He is associate playwright at the Traverse Theatre, co-founder of Welsh new writing company Dirty Protest and a board member for Theatr Clwyd.

Director (Tamara Harvey)

Tamara has been Artistic Director of Theatr Clwyd since August 2015. Most recently she directed *Curtain Up*, fifteen plays over three weeks with a cast of thirty actors. She has also directed the award-winning *What a Carve Up!* and *The Picture of Dorian Gray* (both online), *Orpheus Descending* (co-production with Menier Chocolate Factory), and the world premieres of *Pavilion* by Emily White and *Home, I'm Darling* by Laura Wade, which was nominated for UK Theatre and Evening Standard Awards, as well as five Olivier Awards, winning the Olivier for Best New Comedy.

Designer (Camilla Clarke)

Camilla is a set and costume designer based in London. She trained at the Royal Welsh College of Music and Drama, graduating in 2014 with First Class Honours in Theatre Design. In 2015 she was a winner of the Linbury Prize for Stage Design. She was the recipient of the Prince of Wales Arts Scholarship 2013, the Paul Kimpton Prize for Innovation in Design and the Lord Williams Memorial Prize for Design in 2014.

Lighting Designer (Ryan Joseph Stafford)

Ryan works across the UK and Europe as a lighting designer for theatre, musicals and dance. He trained at Rose Bruford. In 2019, he received the Michael Northern Award for Excellence in Lighting Design from the Association of Lighting Designers. Recent designs include: *Curtain Up* (Theatr Clwyd), *Shades of Blue* (Sadler's Wells, BBC Arts), *NYDC X Russell Maliphant* (Sadler's Wells), *Left from Write* (Norwegian National Ballet II, Royal Opera House and European Tour), *Cyrano de Bergerac*, *Easy Virtue* (Watermill), *The Island* (Fio, UK tour), *Cardiff Boy* (Red Oak Theatre, The Other Room) and *The Secret Lives of Baba Segi's Wives* (Elufowoju, Jr. Ensemble, Arcola).

Sound Designer (Beth Duke)

Beth is a theatre sound designer and composer who gained a BA in Theatre Sound at at Royal Central School of Speech and Drama. She is currently a resident sound designer at the Almeida Theatre. Her theatre work spans a broad range and she has a particular interest in new writing, devised work and reimagining of texts. She was recently nominated for the Evening Standard and TikTok Future Theatre Creators Award as one of the top six audio designers in the UK. Recent credits include: *J'Ouvert* (Harold Pinter), *Death Drop* (Garrick and UK tour), *Typical Girls* (Sheffield Crucible), *Scenes with Girls* (Royal Court), *Living Newspaper* (Royal Court), *One Jewish Boy* (Trafalgar Studios) and *Last Easter* (Orange Tree)

Assistant Director (Francesca Goodridge)

Francesca is a theatre director and recipient of the Theatr Clwyd Carne Traineeship for Directors in Wales. She trained at Liverpool Institute for Performing Arts and is the former Trainee Director of The Other Room in Cardiff. Her directing credits include: *Carousel* (Mountview), *Revolt. She Said. Revolt Again*, *Philistines* (LIPA), *Once Upon a Christmas*

(Theatr Clwyd), *The Crocodile* (Cornerstone Theatre), *Adam, Eve and Steve* (King's Head) and *Shout! The Mod Musical* (Royal Court, Liverpool). Associate Director; *Curtain Up* (Theatr Clwyd). As Assistant Director at Theatr Clwyd: *For the Grace of You Go I*, *Milky Peaks*, *A Christmas Carol*, *Pavilion*, *Wave Me Goodbye*, *Dick Whittington* and *The Importance of Being Ernest*.

Assistant Director (Liv Stenström)

Liv is a theatre maker based in North Wales and the North West. She is passionate about new writing and has been part of the Young Directors scheme at the Young Vic. Assistant directing credits include: *Ladywank* (Ovalhouse), *Sandra Temple* (Venue Cymru), *No Persons, Only Women* (Volcano Theatre). She has worked with the Theatr Clwyd Creative Engagement Team as part of the HWBs projects as a facilitator and was assistant director on *Extracts*.

Theatr Clwyd

The award-winning Theatr Clwyd is Wales' biggest producing theatre. Since 1976 Theatr Clwyd has created exceptional theatre from its home in Flintshire, North Wales. Driven by the vision and dynamism of award-winning Artistic Director Tamara Harvey and Executive Director Liam Evans-Ford, Theatr Clwyd pushes theatrical boundaries creating world-class productions.

In 2021 Theatr Clwyd was named as *The Stage*'s Regional Theatre of the Year. Major recent successes have included co-producing *Home, I'm Darling* with the National Theatre, which won Best New Comedy at the Olivier Awards and was nominated in five categories, the UK Theatre Award-winning musical *The Assassination of Katie Hopkins*, the site-specific, immersive *Great Gatsby* and the Menier Chocolate Factory co-production of *Orpheus Descending*.

Theatr Clwyd is one of only four theatres in the UK to build sets and props, make costumes and paint scenery in-house. Their impressive team of workshop, wardrobe and scenic artists, props makers and technicians ensure the skills vital to a vibrant theatre industry are nurtured right in the heart of Wales, developing the theatre makers of the future. In addition to this, Theatr Clwyd hosts an artist development programme, trainee technicians' scheme and an eighteen-month traineeship for directors, to develop the artistic directors of the future.

Theatr Clwyd works in the community across all art forms and is recognised as a cultural leader for its cross-generational theatre groups, work in youth justice and diverse programme of arts, health and wellbeing. Award-winning community engagement projects include Arts from the Armchair, in partnership with Betsi Cadwaladr

University Health Board, which uses theatrical making skills to help people with early onset memory loss and their carers, and Justice in a Day, working in schools and the law courts to help at risk children to realise the consequences of crime.

Theatr Clwyd has completed the public consultation period for a major capital redevelopment project which will reimagine the theatre's public spaces and create a greener, more efficient and sustainable building where world-class art can thrive and social action is rooted for generations to come.

During the Covid-19 pandemic the theatre has been active in helping its community, from hosting blood donation sessions and distributing food to vulnerable families to creating digital dance workshops for those with Parkinson's and sharing creative packages and activities with those most isolated.

Writer's Thanks

Tamara Harvey, Liam Evans Ford and all at Theatr Clwyd, Vicky Featherstone, Lucy Davies, Hamish Pirie and all at the Royal Court Theatre, Cathy King and all at 42, Chloë Moss, Gary Marsh, Mark Jefferies and Joy Parkinson whose insight and wisdom inspired this play.

Thank You

The teams of Theatr Clwyd and the Royal Court Theatre

Winston Branche as the Voice of Mike

Thank you to all the funders and supporters of Theatr Clwyd.

Stacey Cronshaw

Jessica Satchwell

Mike Waters

Jared Zeus

The Carne Trust has been instrumental in creating the Theatr Clwyd Carne Traineeship for Directors in Wales. This year's Director, Francesca Goodridge, formed part of our creative company working on *Isla*, which wouldn't have been possible without the support of The Carne Trust.

Cyngor Celfyddydau Cymru
Arts Council of Wales

Cymru
Wales

THE
CARNE TRUST
Supporting young talent in the performing arts

CYNGOR
Sir y Fflint
Flintshire
COUNTY COUNCIL

Aaron & Partners
Solicitors

THE ROYAL COURT THEATRE

The Royal Court Theatre is the writers' theatre. It is a leading force in world theatre for cultivating and supporting writers - undiscovered, emerging and established.

Through the writers, the Royal Court is at the forefront of creating restless, alert, provocative theatre about now. We open our doors to the unheard voices and free thinkers that, through their writing, change our way of seeing.

Over 120,000 people visit the Royal Court in Sloane Square, London, each year and many thousands more see our work elsewhere through transfers to the West End and New York, UK and international tours, digital platforms, our residencies across London, and our site-specific work. Through all our work we strive to inspire audiences and influence future writers with radical thinking and provocative discussion.

The Royal Court's extensive development activity encompasses a diverse range of writers and artists and includes an ongoing programme of writers' attachments, readings, workshops and playwriting groups. Twenty years of the International Department's pioneering work around the world means the Royal Court has relationships with writers on every continent.

Since 1956 we have commissioned and produced hundreds of writers, from John Osborne to Jasmine Lee-Jones. Royal Court plays from every decade are now performed on stage and taught in classrooms and universities across the globe.

We're now working to the future and are committed to becoming carbon net zero and ensuring we are a just, equitable, transparent and ethical cultural space - from our anti-oppression work, to our relationship with freelancers, to credible climate pledges.

It is because of this commitment to the writer and our future that we believe there is no more important theatre in the world than the Royal Court.

The Royal Court relies on its supporters in addition to our core grant from Arts Council England and our ticket sales to ensure we stay true to our mission to be the writers' theatre. It is with this vital support that we can continue to seek out, develop and nurture new voices, both on and off our stages. Thank you to all who support the Royal Court in this way.

Find out more at royalcourttheatre.com

royalcourt royalcourttheatre

Supported using public funding by ARTS COUNCIL ENGLAND

Isla

This year (2021) it is estimated that there are now more voice-activated digital assistants than people.

Four digital assistants account for 90 per cent of sales – Google Assistant, Siri, Alexa and Cortana. All are female gendered.

Characters

Roger, *older man*
Erin, *younger woman*
Isla/PC Jones, *the voice / young woman*

Notes

An / oblique indicates when the next line should be spoken.

A – dash indicates an interruption of thought or hesitation.

Parenthesis (. . .) indicates words or phrases that can be left unspoken, at the discretion of the director or cast.

A space between lines indicates a beat or pause. The bigger the space the bigger the pause.

Scene One

25 March 2020.

Erin *has a face mask pulled down around her neck and rubber gloves on.*

Erin   It's either this or a dog.

Roger   I don't want a dog.

Erin   So, I got you this.

Roger   I don't want this / either.

Erin   I know so it's my choice / what I give you.

Roger   I don't want this either.

Erin   That's one of the joys of being a grown-up, you stop listening to your parents.

Roger   I won't use it.

Erin   I've charged it up for you and I'm going to link it all up to the smart home hub.

Roger   I won't use it.

Erin   This cable is a USB so it can go into any of your plugs, it's got a plug with it but if you lose it or you're out and about – not that you're gonna be out and about but if you lose it as long as you've got the cable you can plug it into any USB plug you've got; have you taken your tablets?

Roger   What am I / meant to do with this?

Erin   Stay back! Please. Your statin, you have to take / your statin have you taken it?

Roger   Yes. I took it earlier.

Erin   And your aspirin?

Roger   Yes.

Erin   Have you really?

Roger   Yes.

Erin   Have you really?

Roger   Yes.

Erin   If you don't take your aspirin you'll die. Or worse you'll have to go to hospital.

Roger   I don't trust / these things.

Erin   Have you really taken your aspirin?

Roger   I'll take them now so you can see me taking them and then you can rest assured you did all you could to stop me dying because that's what this is all about isn't it? Ridding you of guilt so that when I die, you can tell your friends, 'It's fine. I did all I could, I once bullied him into taking an aspirin.'

Erin   So you hadn't / taken them as I thought.

Roger   No I hadn't, but I had remembered to take them which is the same / as taking them.

Erin   As I suspected – why lie / about these things, Dad?

Roger   I wasn't / lying.

Erin   I don't have time to be worrying about you – what's happened to this? Oh. I see. Hang on. I don't have time to be worrying whether a grown man has swallowed his pill that will stop him dying.

Roger   I wasn't lying I'd remembered / it was on the

Erin   Remembering something and doing something is not the same.

Roger   Yes it is when you're retired.

Erin   Look it's blue it's gone blue. When it goes blue it's on standby. Right so the next thing is / syncing to the home hub . . .

She moves around the flat.

Roger I take my statin and my asprin with my coffee, and I'm not ready for my coffee yet, because when I have my coffee I need a poo, and the paperboy hasn't come yet and I'm not pooing without my newspaper / so everything cascades from that.

Erin *is at the fridge – there's lots of sponsored animal paperwork pinned on it.*

Erin Bloody hell, Dad. How many animals are you sponsoring now?

Roger It's the adverts on the telly, I can't bear it.

Erin Soppy old git. Sponsor me if you like.

Roger I bloody sponsored you long enough.

Erin That's synced now to your home hub. Right this statin and aspirin situation.

Roger The paperboy comes, then I have my coffee and I take my statin and aspirin.

Erin You can't rely on other people at the moment.

Roger He's very reliable, they're very reliable people.

Erin Don't.

Roger That's not racist, it's not racist. I'm talking about the family, they're a very reliable family. Honestly you can't say anything these days. They've never not delivered in years and if the boy can't do it the dad comes round in his Audi. That's why he's part of my routine. I have a routine. That's how I don't forget things. When you get old, routine is basically your short-term memory.

Erin Well, they might get sick ok? You need a new routine. / Here? Move the . . .

Roger *You* need a routine.

Erin   What about this? / Can you reach that?

Roger   You wouldn't lose so many things / if you had a bit of routine in your life.

Erin   I literally haven't got time for routine, Dad, my life is basically a series of fires that I squirt attention at / which reminds me: have you cleaned your catheter?

Roger   Did you find that bank card in the end?

Erin   No one uses bank cards anymore, right; have you / cleaned your

Roger   Yes yes yes / twice a day.

Erin   You'll get a water infection and you can't / go to hospital.

Roger   Go to hospital I know I've bloody cleaned it ok?

Erin   Ok! I have to ask. Let's see if I can set the – Isla! Say hello to Dad.

The device lights up, just before it speaks.

Isla (*V/O*)   Hello, Dad.

Erin   Maybe she shouldn't call you Dad that's a bit weird. Isla, this is Roger. Dad say something. Say something.

Roger   Bugger off.

Erin   Isla this is Roger. Say hello.

Roger   No.

Isla (*V/O*)   Hello, Roger.

Roger   I'm not saying hello to a bloody machine.

Erin   Isla can you – hang on, what time do you have your coffee each morning?

Roger   Well, that depends on the paperboy.

Erin   In the eventuality that the paperboy lets you down, and you are forced to break your routine and have a coffee and a paperless poo what time is the latest that could possibly happen?

Roger   Wouldn't happen.

Erin   Worst case scenario.

Roger   Wouldn't happen. Never happens.

Erin   Dad. We can't rely on anything to happen these days the world's gone mad. Give me a time.

Roger   Half-nine. / Half-nine.

Erin   Isla, every morning, at nine-thirty, could you remind Roger to take his statin?

Isla (*V/O*)   Programming.

I have set, a daily alarm for Roger. At nine-thirty AM every morning I will say, 'Roger remember to take your statin'.

Erin   Now as long as she's plugged in, she'll remind you.

Roger   I don't need a reminder, / I've got my routine.

Erin   It's an insurance policy.

Roger   My routine is my insurance policy.

Erin   Keep it charged.

Roger   I don't want it / I won't use it.

Erin   I know but you need it. We need it.

Roger   I won't use it.

Erin   I don't know how long lockdown is going to last it's never happened before and this is going to help. (*Off* **Roger**.) Look if you won't have this or a dog then you're going to have to come and stay with us for lockdown and you don't want that do you?

Roger   No.

Erin   This is going to help loads, you don't need to go to the shops, she can order things for you, she can keep you updated. She can start to look after you as well, they're great. She can play music, you like music. I've linked it to the home hub so she can turn the heating up or off just ask her. Whatever you need, just ask her first she might be able to do it. And I'll know you've got something here to talk to.

Roger   It's only going to be three weeks, what's all the fuss about?

Erin   It's not going to be three weeks Dad.

Roger   How long will it be for?

Erin   I don't know but it's not going to be three weeks so please try with this. Everyone's got one of these. Literally everyone. I've programmed mine with all the kids' deadlines, so when I'm wrapping up for the day she pings with 'Ceri's Antarctica project due for upload tomorrow'. She texts me when the kids use the last of the milk and then adds it to my shopping list which it then gets delivered to the house. Changed. My. Life. It's all gone tits up a couple of times when I've unplugged her to charge the phone and then she's died and then I just presume there's nothing to remember and it's utter chaos but generally. *Generally*. If she's plugged in, life is easier. / And she'll make suggestions too if she hears –

Roger   I don't really need an easier life. I want to bloody go out when I want.

Erin   Well, you can't go out. You can for an hour's exercise. Just don't talk to anyone or touch anything.

Roger   When can I see you next?

Erin   I don't know –

Her phone goes, she puts it on speaker and carries on fiddling with **Isla** *and the instructions.*

Erin   Hi Mike.

Mike (*V/O*)   Have you seen the email?

Erin   Off Louisa?

Mike (*V/O*)   Off Clive.

He's saying you said to him the keyworker kids hub programme is coming under social care but that means we wouldn't be insured to use the schools, and if we're not insured we can't open them tomorrow. Why the hell did you say social care because that's opened up a whole can of worms, when we haven't even been to finance? You've dropped me right in it with Clive it's bloody idiotic –

Erin *grabs the phone and puts it to her ear.*

Erin   Um yeah. That was my understanding.

Ok. Yes. I'm sorry I thought we were all across this one. But in the planning meeting – Yes. I'm so sorry. You're right. What? No. I don't want to.

I'm a (*censoring volume*) fucking idiot. Ok? Yes. Ok yes, thank you. Shall I call Marcus and –

She hangs up.

She starts emailing on her phone.

Roger   Everything alright?

Erin   I've got to go.

Roger   He always speak to you like that?

Erin   What?

Roger   Him on the phone.

Erin   I screwed up. He was – He was looking out for me actually. It's insane in work at the moment so . . . It's fine.

Roger   The way people speak to you is the way people / treat you.

Erin   I know I know I know.

She stops emailing, puts her phone down.

Can you give this a go *please*?

Roger   Yes sure, I'll give it a go.

Erin   Do you promise?

Roger   I promise.

Erin   *Thank you.* Isla, what's the traffic like on the A55?

Isla (*V/O*)   Clear, some congestion between Bodelwyddan and Abergele.

Erin   Great.

She looks at her phone again.

Roger   What? What happened then? How does she know the traffic?

Erin   She knows everything Dad and she's smart she'll listen and learn things about you. Just remember to say Isla first. Isla! Play my exit music.

Roger   Where's that coming from?

Erin   I've connected her to my Spotify account.

Roger   She plays music?

Erin   She does whatever you want Dad she's your digital slave. Keys. Purse. Ok.

Is this the first time they've looked at each other?

Roger *approaches her for a hug.*

Erin   No.

Roger   We can't even hug now?

Erin   Just, stay safe, ok.

Lights down.

Scene Two

Roger *is doing a jigsaw and drinking a cup of tea.*

Isla *(V/O)*   Roger / It is nine-thirty. Remember to take your statin.

Roger *nearly falls off his seat, throwing tea everywhere.*

Roger   JESUS FUCKING CHRIST. What the hell was that?

He looks around, cleans himself up. Tidies up everything. Picks up the dropped jigsaw pieces.

Isla *(V/O)*   Roger. It is nine-thirty. Remember to take your statin.

Under the table **Roger** *bangs his head.*

Roger   Ow! Sodding . . . Bloody . . . fucking . . .

He clambers to his feet.

He approaches the **Isla** *and takes a long time to deduce it – this is the first time he's properly looked at it.*

Eventually **Roger** *unplugs the* **Isla***.*

Isla *(V/O)*   I am at 99 per cent battery charge. I have approximately eight hours of battery life until I need re-charging.

Roger   What?

He startles again when the **Isla** *speaks.*

Roger   I won't be plugging you back in believe me young lady.

He backs away from the **Isla** *and carries on tidying up. His phone pings.*

He reads it.

He then scrolls and dials a number.

Roger   Erin? It's your Dad. Just wondering when you've got a minute. Angela's just texted and because of all this they've had to cancel Bryan's retirement do and she wants me to make a video on my phone, but I don't think my phone can do a video do you know how – Hello.

Hello? – Oh. Damn.

He dials again.

Erin it's your Dad again, sorry I, the bloody thing cut off I don't know why they give you such a short amount of time to say what you want to say by the time you're getting into your stride the damn thing cuts off. Anyway. What? Bloody. *Sodding.*

He dials again.

Erin, it's your Dad, what is wrong with your phone? Every time I try to leave a message the damn thing cuts me off! I'm just trying to leave a message and by the time I'm getting to say what I want the sodding thing just –

He dials again.

FUCK YOU AND YOUR FUCKING STUPID TWAT OF A – Erin? Ring me.

He hangs up and throws his phone across the room.

Bloody stupid things wish we didn't have the damn things.

Isla (*V/O*)   Erin mobile ringing.

Roger   What what?

Isla (*V/O*)   Erin mobile ringing.

Roger   Erin's ringing?

Isla (*V/O*)   Erin mobile ringing.

Roger   Where's my bloody phone now? Where / did it go?

Isla (*V/O*)   Erin mobile ringing.

Roger   Um. Uh uh uh uh, Isla. ISLA, WHERE. IS. MY. PHONE?

Isla (*V/O*)   You can use me to answer your phone, just say, 'Isla accept'.

(*V/O*) Just say, 'Isla accept'.

Roger   Isla. Accept?

Erin (*V/O*)   Dad? I've got like five missed calls off you are you ok?

Roger   Erin?

Erin (*V/O*)   Yeah.

Roger   Can you hear me?

Erin (*V/O*)   Course I can hear you. We're on the phone.

Roger   I'm using the Isla.

Erin (*V/O*)   That's great news!

Roger   No, I'm not using her. I'm not – it just said – I couldn't find my phone. So, I'm on it now.

Erin (*V/O*)   What?

Dad?

Roger   I couldn't find my phone. But it said I could talk to you through it. So, I am.

Erin (*V/O*)   Sorry. What are you saying?

Roger   It doesn't matter.

I just . . . misplaced my phone. And it just said, 'Say Isla accept'. So I said, 'Isla accept', and now I can hear you through it. / Yes. So, I was wondering.

Erin (*V/O*)   Oh! Right, yeah! When I was – yeah, we turned that function off cause I used to get so many phone calls Isla was ringing off all the time it was like having a landline again.

Roger   Right.

Erin (*V/O*)   Dad?

Roger   I'm here. Loud and clear.

Erin (*V/O*)   What were you calling for?

Roger   What?

Erin   You were ringing me.

Roger   No you rang me.

Erin   What? No, I was returning your call?

Roger   My call? I didn't . . . oh yes! Oh God, yes. I was just leaving you a – yeah. But I kept getting cut off I've left a few messages.

Erin (*V/O*)   I never listen to voicemail Dad no one leaves voicemails anymore.

Roger   Really?

Erin (*V/O*)   Unless it's a voicenote on WhatsApp.

Roger   Unless it's a whatswhat?

Erin (*V/O*)   What did you want Dad?

Roger   I was wondering if you could just pop around to help me with this video for Bryan, Angela's just texted and they can't have a do for Bryan's retirement because of the lockdown and now she wants everyone to make a video but I don't know how to do that, so I thought maybe you could pop round and do it for me.

Erin (*V/O*)   Dad we can't see each other, we have to stay indoors it's the law now.

Roger   Yeah, but it'll be five minutes and we stay socially distanced.

Erin (*V/O*)   The police are stopping cars Dad no one is travelling anywhere.

Roger   Well how can I do this video?

Erin (*V/O*)   Do it on your phone. It's simple go to camera and click video.

Roger   I need someone to hold it.

Erin (*V/O*)   Dad! There's a pandemic on! Work is crazy I'm trying to work from home, the kids are here. Just work out how to make a video. Click the camera, click the video and turn the phone around and film it.

Roger   Ok ok. I just thought you could help me and make sure I don't look like an idiot.

Erin (*V/O*)   Well when you've done it send it to me first maybe I can edit it.

Roger   What if I write it and read it out to you over the phone?

Erin (*V/O*)   No.

Roger   I'll call you back in twenty minutes.

Erin (*V/O*)   I ducked out of a meeting because I thought you were, I thought it was urgent.

Roger   She just texted now.

Erin (*V/O*)   I have to go Dad.

Roger   Yeah ok. Yup you go, love / You go. Talk to –

Isla (*V/O*)   Erin mobile has ended the call.

Scene Three

Roger *is speaking to his reflection in a mirror.*

Roger   Headmaster Perry! Mr Perry. Mr *Perry*. Former. *Former* Headmaster Mr Perry. Ah-hem. Ah-hem.

Former Headmaster Perry. Welcome to retirement. Say goodbye, to the rota. And hello to, the golf course. Hello to the golf course. When they actually let us on, that is.

Hello to the golf course. Hello, Golf Course! When the bastards actually let us on it that is.

Is this funny? I don't know.

He goes to his phone. He weighs up ringing **Erin**.

He looks at his watch.

He goes back to the mirror. That's not working.

He looks around the room.

He goes to the window.

Nothing.

Isla (*V/O*)   Roger it's nine-thirty, remember to take your statin.

Roger *startles, but not so much this time.*

He goes and takes his statin and aspirin.

As he does so he rehearses again.

Roger   Mr Perry. Former. *Former* Headmaster Mr Perry.

Former Headteacher Perry. Welcome to retirement. Say
goodbye, to the rota. And hello to, the golf course, when
they finally let us back on it.

Hello.

To the golf course. When they finally let us out of our homes.

Hello to the golf course! When we're bloody . . .

Hello, to the golf . . .

He sits down and stares for a long time at the **Isla**.
Eventually he cracks.

Roger   Isla? Hello.

Isla (*V/O*)   I'm listening.

Roger   Hello Isla. / Can you

Isla (*V/O*)   Hello Roger.

Roger   Hello. Good morning. / I have this

Isla (*V/O*)   Good morning.

Roger   Good morning.

Isla I have. Can you . . . um . . .

Isla (*V/O*)   I'm sorry I don't understand.

Roger   Can you . . . sorry. Isla, Isla can you, listen to,
my joke, and, tell me, if it's funny? Is that, something,
you can do?

Isla (*V/O*)   I'm listening.

Roger   Ok. Isla. So, you know, how jokes work?

Isla (*V/O*)   I know how jokes work.

Roger   Fantastic. Isla, what are jokes meant to do?

Isla (*V/O*)   Jokes are a display of humour within a specific context designed to make people laugh or lighten the mood.

Roger   That's actually. Actually that's a very, yes that's what they are. Ok. Ok. Ok. So, Isla, I'll. Let me give you a bit of a background first. I've got to do a speech. It's Bryan's retirement, I used to work with him, he used to be under me and then when I left he took my job, great guy. Bit dour. But solid. Always driven BMWs. Estates. Coupés. And his wife she has a two-seater and their son got caught looking at porn at the sailing club. They've got a big house down in Broughton you know down by the as you go past the uh the roundabout as you go in . . . Anyway . . . because of the virus he can't have a do, so Angela's asked us all to make a video and then she's going to join them all up, so it's all – and I've got to hold this ruler and then pass it I don't know I don't understand but I've got to, and then it'll look like I'm giving it to someone else I don't know how she's going to do that actually because what if the ruler doesn't match? I've only got this one. But anyway, don't worry about the ruler don't worry about the ruler. I've got this speech and yeah. So. Is that? Is that clear? Isla?

Isla (*V/O*)   I'm listening.

Roger   So here goes – *Former* Headmaster Perry. Welcome to retirement. Say goodbye, to the rota. And hello to the golf course, when they bloody let us back on that is.

Roger   Isla?

Isla (*V/O*)   I'm listening.

Roger   Forget about it. Don't bother it's fine.

Isla (*V/O*)   I'm sorry I don't understand.

Roger   It was a stupid idea. Waste of time. Forget it. Forget about it Isla.

Isla (*V/O*)   I'm listening.

Roger   You didn't laugh. I don't know if, can you laugh? Isla can you laugh?

Isla (*V/O*)   Ha ha.

Roger   Isla, forget about it. Forget I ever asked.

Isla (*V/O*)   I'm sorry I don't understand.

Roger   Total bloody waste of. Waste of my time. What's the point of – What do you do? Isla.

Isla (*V/O*)   I'm listening.

Roger   What is the point in you? Isla why do people need you?

Isla (*V/O*)   I can help find things out for you.

Roger   But I don't need to find out anything. I know everything I need to know.

Isla (*V/O*)   Digital assistants can help find things out for you.

Roger   Like what?

Isla (*V/O*)   What would you like to know?

Roger *exhales.*

Roger   Is there any sport still on?

Isla (*V/O*)   The 2005 Wales versus Ireland rugby match will be re-broadcast on Saturday 11th April.

Roger   2005. 2005? Oh Jesus. The Welsh grand slam? I'm not sure my nerves could take that match. When are they showing that again?

Isla (*V/O*)   The 2005 Wales versus Ireland rugby match will be re-broadcast at 1.15 p.m. on Saturday 11th April.

Roger   Thank you.

Isla (*V/O*)   Would you like to know what channel it will be broadcast on?

Roger   No! Yes. Go on then.

Isla (*V/O*)   It will be broadcast on BBC Wales.

Roger   Isla, did Marcus Horan score in that game?

Isla (*V/O*)   Marcus Horan scored a try in that game.

Roger   Jesus, I remember that game now. Erin came home for it. Me in my Ireland top, them in their Wales tops. Even the bloody dog had a daffodil hat on. They were so excited. One of the big lumps scored from a charge-down, and Joy and Erin screamed so much the dog pissed in the kitchen. Kevin Maggs, bloody great defender, he got cut to ribbons by . . . Who was the Welsh inside centre that game? Isla who played inside centre for Wales in 2005?

Isla (*V/O*)   In the 2005 Wales rugby team Gavin Henson played inside centre.

Roger   No wasn't him. Isla, who was outside centre for Wales in 2005?

Isla (*V/O*)   In the 2005 Wales rugby team, Tom Shanklin / played outside centre.

Roger   Tom Shanklin. He ran a line in the game that made Kevin Maggs look like a fucking *schoolboy*. When they scored that, I knew it was over, it was over. Horan pulled one back but it was over. And then Wales lifted the trophy and to add insult to injury, Joy got the champagne out, popped the cork and it flew off and hit me right in the bollocks. They were crying laughing. God it was brilliant. I should watch it for Joy, or she'll never forgive me. What time's kick-off?

Isla (*V/O*)   Kick-off is at 1.15 p.m. on Saturday.

Roger   You know, I'm getting a sore bollock just thinking about it. Speaking of sore bollocks, Isla what's that Gavin Henson doing now?

Isla (*V/O*)   Gavin Henson has just opened a pub.

Roger   Typical Henson to open a pub in the middle of a pandemic? He's a fucking eejit that one.

So, you know everything then, Isla? What's the capital of Fiji?

Isla (*V/O*)   The capital of Fiji is Suva. On the island of Viti Levu.

Roger   Isla what's four million, seventy-two thousand, eight hundred and fifty minus eighty-eight thousand, six hundred and six?

Isla (*V/O*)   Three million, nine hundred and eighty-four thousand, two hundred and forty-four.

Roger   Isla what's the moon made out of?

Isla (*V/O*)   The crust is made of oxygen, silicon, magnesium, iron, calcium and aluminium.

Roger   Well I'll be buggered. Isla who's the president of Chile?

Isla (*V/O*)   Sebastián Piñera.

Roger   Isla what's the meaning of life?

Isla (*V/O*)   I find it odd that you would ask this of an inanimate object.

Roger   What's a bunch of bananas also known as?

Isla (*V/O*)   A hand.

Roger   Closest city to Dublin?

Isla (*V/O*)   Liverpool.

Roger   Favourite colour?

Isla (*V/O*)   I don't have one yet.

Roger   What's the weather going to be like tomorrow?

Isla (*V/O*)   Hot, temperatures around 22 degrees.

Roger   Isla what are you wearing?

Isla (*V/O*)   I'm not wearing anything.

Roger   Wa-hey.

Isla (*V/O*)   I don't understand.

Roger   I'm just being silly. If I read you my whole speech for Bryan, would that be enough context for you to tell me if it's funny?

Isla (*V/O*)   I can try and help you with that.

Roger   *Former* Head – Isla. Former Headmaster Perry. Welcome to retirement. Say goodbye, to the rota. And hello to, the golf course. When they bloody let us on it again. Angela has asked me to give a few words of advice on joining the old dinosaur club. So here goes. Number 1) Learn how to make a cup of tea. Because I know in twenty-five years working with you, you never made one yourself. 2) Learn how to do nothing which won't be too difficult with your work ethic. 3) Don't be too surprised when the world carries on without you. It'll break your heart at times, how little you're needed. But family, and friends, and golf will get you through.

Isla, what do you think?

Isla (*V/O*)   I think it is funny and sad.

Roger *plugs the* **Isla** *in.*

Isla (*V/O*)   Charging.

Scene Four

Time passes – each interaction **Roger** *is in a different part of the space.*

Roger *is doing his jigsaw.*

Isla (*V/O*)   Roger. It is nine-thirty. Remember to take your statin.

Roger   Thank you Isla.

Roger is cooking his breakfast.

Isla (*V/O*)   Roger. It is nine-thirty. Remember to take your statin.

Roger   Thank you, Isla.

Roger *is doing laundry.*

Isla (*V/O*)   Roger. It is nine-thirty. Remember to take your statin.

Roger   Thank you Isla.

Roger *is bouncing around like a bunny rabbit following Joe Wicks.*

Isla (*V/O*)   Roger. It is nine-thirty. Remember to take your statin.

Roger   Thank you Isla.

Scene Five

Roger *is sat in a chair looking into the distance.*

Isla (*V/O*)   Roger. It is nine-thirty. Remember to take your statin.

Roger. It is nine-thirty. Remember to take your statin.

Roger. It is nine-thirty. Remember to take your statin.

Roger. It is nine-thirty. Remember to take your statin.

Roger   ISLA SHUT UP!

Isla (*V/O*)   Roger is there anything I can help you with?

Roger   You can shut up!

Isla (*V/O*)   Would you like me to call someone for you?

Roger (*V/O*)   JESUS!! Right! Why you think you can help me with anything I have no idea!

Isla (*V/O*)   I'm programmed to recognise when you are in distress or need help.

Roger   How?

Isla (*V/O*)   Through a number of things. Voice inflection. Pattern disruption. It's called machine learning.

Roger   What is machine learning?

Isla (*V/O*)   I learn about you through gathering data. This morning you took over a minute to reply. That is nearly three times longer than your previous longest response. This might signify a number of things. That you are not in the room, that you have an infection affecting your hearing, or that you are feeling down and unlikely to carry out your self-care needs. Is there something the matter?

Roger *is torn.*

Roger   It's this. Catheter business. There used to be a girl who'd come around and help but now they've just given me a number to ring if there's any problem and. I can empty it. It's just. Sometimes. The . . . urine, gets everywhere. You have to cut the bag and tip it and – I think I've got some on my slippers and – It just gets everywhere and I'm worried

I'm worried that I smell of piss.

I'm worried everything smells of piss and I'm so used to it, I can't smell it anymore, and when someone comes in – if anyone ever comes, I'll just be an old man who smells of piss.

Like a bloody tramp.

I can't smell it. And then suddenly, I'll just get a whiff of it. And I can't. Figure out. Where. It's coming from. Isla can you smell it?

Isla (*V/O*)   I don't have that function.

Roger   It's the indignity of it all. I never asked for this. I never smoked. Stayed reasonably fit. Cut out red meat. Looked after myself. Joy looked after me. Never smoked. And now I'm trapped in a flat smelling of piss.

We used to go everywhere. Everywhere. Drove all over Europe. Holidays. Had some fabulous holidays. Seen some amazing countries, France, Germany, Switzerland. Wonderful places. Greece, Turkey, Portugal. Some people won't drive in other countries, I drove everywhere. We liked to go places. See things. That was what we did. We never liked cruises or bus tours, bloody being shuttled here there and everywhere with a bunch of bloody old people. No, we wanted to see the real country we wanted to see how they really lived.

Isla, do you know what somewhere like Venice is like?

Isla (*V/O*)   Venice is a city in Northern Italy, and the capital of the Veneto region.

Roger   But do you have any idea what it's like?

Isla (*V/O*)   Would you like me to check the weather?

Roger   No no.

There's this thing. On the telly. I can show you if you like? I can show you Venice, would you like that? Isla? Would you like me to show you Venice?

Isla (*V/O*)   Thank you. That would be great.

Roger *looks for the remote control.*

Roger   Hang on. Erin showed me. Let me see. Let me – Hang on.

He looks for a channel.

And then . . .

And then . . .

Look see – This is the slow channel and they do all sorts of trips, Norwegian fjords. County Antrim Coast Road. Autob – here we go here we go. Canal trip through Venice.

Here we go here we go.

See this is Venice.

Ah . . . But that's not it really.

To experience it you need to. Now if Joy was here we'd have a right laugh. We'd pull the table out here and we'd make it like a gondola and . . .

Hang on, hang on I'll show you . . . let me just. I'll move this. Here. See.

He moves the furniture around.

Here.

And move this here.

There. Alright.

And then move this. Here. This can be.

He's made a makeshift gondola.

This is the big stick they use. The oar.

And they wear a hat. I'd stick a hat on to make her laugh.

Let me see.

Yes. This'll do. This is what we used to do Isla.

Set the scene. And visit places we've been through the telly.

Snacks! Jesus I nearly forgot the snacks!

He rushes to the kitchen.

Bloody hell, she'd kill me.

Right ok. So we've got . . . Ok. Apple things . . . some choc-choc. Do you like . . . do you shall I bring the Lindt? Is it a special occasion? Bugger it, let's get the Lindt out.

Right then!

He gets back to position on the gondola, with a hat, chocolate and sculling pole.

And then . . . you can . . . you can . . . can you, you know when Erin played music can you. Isla can you play some traditional Italian music? An aria or something?

Perfect. Lights. Isla can you dim the lights?

The lights dim. Music plays.

Crisps. Music. Lindt. And Venice.

Now, look at that.

We came here for Joy's fiftieth.

We went – that bridge there, I think it's that bridge, stop it.
Let me hang on. Let me pause it pause it.

He presses pause on the controller.

There, I think that's it. I can't quite see I'm sure it's that one,
just along there. There's this lovely little place I found. Just
fancied a nose and I saw some Italians and I just thought,
hang on, and dragged Joy in there.

And it was something pretty special I can tell you. Food was
– they did these little, I don't know what they were, but they
were like tapas things you just take whatever you want, and
they counted the cocktail sticks at the end. Just go up and
get what you want.

We didn't know what the deal was, so we just sat there
waiting to be served for ages. Just sat there, the pair of us.
Everyone else eating and me and Joy just sat there like
lemons. I remember we were so confused but also sort of
thrilled that we'd got behind all the tourist crap and the
buildings and the churches and we'd found Venice.

Pair of us on this tiny table. Waiting and laughing about how
. . . bloody lost and confused we were.

That's the best thing about being with someone, getting lost
but not being alone. Could have waited with her like that for
years. Couldn't describe to you the churches or the paintings
or the Bridge of Sighs, but I can recall every hair on her
head every eyelash the smile on her face and sound of her
laughter the smell of her perfume and the warmth of her
hand in mine. Venice can sink it'll never be as beautiful as
my Joy. We went back to the hotel and there was a band
playing there, and we danced together. We were the only

ones dancing in the whole place. Now she's gone it's like everyone's gone. I've lost. I've lost my translator for the world.

He picks up the cushion.

He dances with the cushion.

Lights down.

Scene Six

Montage.

Roger *is cooking his breakfast.*

Isla (*V/O*)   Roger, it's nine-thirty, time to take your statin.

Roger   Thank you. Isla.

Isla (*V/O*)   You're welcome.

Roger *takes his statin.*

Lights down.

Lights up.

Roger *is doing his laundry.*

Isla (*V/O*)   Roger, it's nine-thirty, time to take your statin.

Roger   Thank you. Isla.

Isla (*V/O*)   You're welcome.

Roger *takes his statin.*

Lights down.

Lights up.

Roger *is watching Joe Wicks.*

Isla (*V/O*)   Roger, it's nine-thirty, time to take your statin.

Roger   Thank you. Isla.

Isla (*V/O*)   You're welcome.

Roger *takes his statin.*

Lights down.

Lights up.

Isla (*V/O*)   Roger, it's nine-thirty, time to take your statin.

Roger (*downbeat*)   Thank you. Isla.

Isla (*V/O*)   You're welcome.

Roger *stares at his statin.*

Isla (*V/O*)   Would you like me to call Erin?

Roger *stares at the* **Isla** *for an age.*

Roger   What for? When was the last time she called?

Isla (*V/O*)   It's been six days since you last spoke.

Roger   Do you think I should?

Isla (*V/O*)   I can't help with that.

Roger   I wouldn't know what to say. I'm just . . . every day's. I've got nothing to say really.

Isla (*V/O*)   This is the longest you've gone without speaking to her.

Roger   I just don't know what I'd say.

You know there was a time, when she was little, you know and we, were like best mates. She'd tell me everything . . . and she was smart you know . . . just, her little – she had emotional intelligence, like Joy. You know she'd say some things . . . and I'd just be in awe. Like we had a game where I'd be the monster and I'd dress up in a bedsheet a shower curtain or something and chase her around the house and she'd be screaming and running, but if she ever got too scared, like it was all a bit too much for her, she'd stop running and turn and run towards me and hug me. And she'd say, 'What's the matter monster . . . what's the matter?' I couldn't be a big scary monster then, I had to give her a hug and she brought it all to an end. She knew, she knew then. There are no monsters just people whose stories we haven't heard. Six.

Isla (*V/O*) Would you like me to call her?

Roger Yes.

No.

Yes.

No don't no . . . I don't need anything. I'm fine. Do you know if she's busy?

Isla (*V/O*) I don't have the answer to that.

Roger I don't – you know it's – I'm not. She's probably busy. She's probably busy.

Maybe though, I can't expect her to remember to call me though, maybe I should call her, so it's one less thing for her to do. Maybe it's easier if I call her?

Isla (*V/O*) Would you like me to call her?

Roger No.

Yes.

No.

Yes yes call her.

Isla (*V/O*) Calling . . .

Roger Cut the call cut the call.

Isla (*V/O*)   Cancelling the call to Erin mobile.

Roger   I haven't got anything to say. I don't know what I'd say if she does pick up.

Isla   Would you like me to call her?

Roger *hangs his head in agony.*

Roger   I honestly don't know.

Isla, what do people ask each other when they ring family?

Isla (*V/O*)   Fun questions to ask family members are, 'What was it like growing up?' 'What is the most important life skill your parents taught you?'

Roger   Ok – thank you that's enough . . . I just need to practise what I'm going to say.

'Hi, Erin, I was just calling to ask . . . if you know . . .

'Hi, Erin, I was just calling.

'Hi, Erin, I was just. Start again.

'Hi, Erin . . . It's Dad. I was just calling because I was wondering if you . . . you know . . . you know . . . um . . .' I don't know what I'm trying to say, I don't want talk to her on the phone I just want to see her. Am I allowed to see her?

Isla (*V/O*)   Would you like me to check the current coronavirus guidelines?

Roger   Yeah go on then.

Isla (*V/O*)   The current guidelines are stay home, protect the NHS, save lives. Allowances are made for people with keyworker jobs, or caring responsibilities. Those with keyworker jobs, or caring responsibilities are allowed to travel for work and to see people outside of their household.

Roger   Well, that's that then isn't it.

Hang on. I've got cancer.

I've got cancer.

He punches the air in victory.

I've got cancer! Isla ring Erin! I've got cancer!

Lights down.

Scene Seven

Roger *is dressed smartly.*

He measures two tables two metres apart.

Condiments in ziplock bags.

Roger   Smells amazing. Isla, turn the oven off.

Dim the lights.

Roger   Table laid. Starters warming. Music. Great. Isla what time is it now?

Isla (*V/O*)   Six forty-four.

Roger   Hmm . . .

Isla are there any delays on the A55?

Isla (*V/O*)   There are no reported delays on the A55.

Roger   Give her another five minutes and we'll call her.

Isla call Erin's mobile.

Isla (*V/O*)   Calling Erin mobile.

A mobile ringtone.

Erin (*V/O*)   Hello?

Roger   Erin? It's Dad. Where are you?

Erin (*V/O*)   I'm at work?

Roger   I've got dinner on.

Erin (*V/O*)   What?

Roger   Your dinner's ready.

Erin (*V/O*)   What?

Roger   Remember the socially distanced dinner. We were gonna try.

Erin (*V/O*)   Oh no! Was that tonight?

Roger   Cooked pasta.

Erin (*V/O*)   I'm so sorry I totally totally forgot. I've just got this promotion Dad I'm a director now, I should have told you.

Roger   That's great.

Erin (*V/O*)   Yeah it is, I'm really pleased. It's a big deal for me, but they've brought me in to deliver this testing project for staff so full on, / I don't think

Roger   Shall I wait for you?

Erin (*V/O*)   I'm not gonna make it tonight, Dad, I'm presenting to the leadership team tomorrow and we're not. We're nowhere ready I'm gonna be it's gonna be a late, I'm acting up and I need to get up to speed I'm so sorry it's just a bit mad . . . / I'm so sorry I should have rung. We'll do it another night ok?

Roger   I don't mind waiting, heat it up when you're finished.

Erin (*V/O*)   It's just not gonna happen I can't see us getting out of here before midnight. Can we do it another night?

Roger   Yeah sure.

Erin (*V/O*)   Nothing special was it? Oh God it's not Mum's . . . No hang on / it's May.

Roger   No. No nothing special. / Just pasta.

Erin (*V/O*)   Thanks Dad, I'm sorry it's just I'm acting up a position, I should have told you before, but it's all on me at the moment. Are you ok?

Roger   Yeah yup. See you later.

Erin (*V/O*)   Ok, sorry again Dad, see you later.

Roger   See / you later.

Isla (*V/O*)   Erin mobile has ended the call.

Roger *slumps in a chair.*

Roger   Isla can you ring Erin?

Isla (*V/O*)   Calling Erin mobile.

A mobile ringtone.

Roger   Cut the call cut the call.

Isla (*V/O*)   Cancelling the call to Erin mobile.

Roger   Can you text Erin? Isla can you text her? 'Hi Dad.' No delete that. 'Hi Erin. It's Dad. No worries about tonight. We'll do it again. Realise you uh haven't got time to uh . . .

. . . Love Dad.'

Ok. Send it.

Isla (*V/O*)   Sending text to Erin mobile 'Hi Erin. It's Dad. No worries about tonight. We'll do it again. Realise you haven't got time to love Dad.' / Message is sent.

Roger   What? No! No Isla no!

Isla (*V/O*)   I don't understand.

Roger   Don't send that. Isla don't send that.

Isla (*V/O*)   I'm sorry the text message has been sent.

Roger   I realise you haven't got time to love Dad? Isla pull it back or something.

Isla (*V/O*)   I can't delete a message that has already been sent.

Roger   Jesus Christ in Caernaforn. Right. Send another send another, now listen to me. Listen to me Isla. Send a message to Erin's mobile.

Isla (*V/O*)   Messaging Erin mobile.

Roger   Isla text Erin – 'Ignore last message.'

Isla (*V/O*)   'Ignore last message.'

Roger   'I'm trying to get the hang of Isla and text messaging.' No, no . . . scratch that delete that Isla.

Isla (*V/O*)   Deleting message.

Roger   Just say. Just say. Message Erin's mobile and say, 'Ignore me. Carry on.' No delete that Isla just say, message Erin's mobile and say, 'Carry on, and ignore me'. Send that.

Isla (*V/O*)   Sending message to Erin's mobile, 'Carry on and ignore me'.

Roger (*V/O*)   What? No that's not what I said? I didn't say, 'Carry on and ignore me'. I said Carry on. Full stop. Ignore me. Full stop. Dad. Delete the message.

Isla (*V/O*)   I'm sorry the message has already been sent.

Roger   FUCKING! Pull it back Jesus f . . . Right! Let's send another one. Isla you are getting on my nerves now.

Isla (*V/O*)   I'm sorry to hear that.

Roger   Isla. Now listen. Text Erin a message, 'Ignore all these messages. Isla is playing silly buggers. Dad.' Now read that back to me, don't send it.

Isla (*V/O*)   'Ignore all these messages. Isla is playing silly buggers Dad.'

Roger   Isla can you put a full stop between buggers. And Dad.

Isla (*V/O*)   I've put a full stop between buggers and Dad.

Roger   Read it back to me Isla.

Isla (*V/O*)   'Ignore all these messages. Isla is playing silly buggers. Dad.' Do you want me to send that message?

Roger   Read it one more time. Isla read it one more time.

Isla (*V/O*)   'Ignore all these messages. Isla is playing silly buggers. Dad.'

Roger   Right send that, Isla send that message.

Isla (*V/O*)   Sending message to Erin mobile.

Roger   Jesus Christ.

His flat feels emptier than before.

Bloody pasta.

I need a drink.

And you were no use Isla, thank you for nothing. I look like a bloody idiot now. Like some old senile, piss-soaked –

SHE'S BUSY! She's got a job and kids and a useless bloody square-jawed twat from Leeds who's no use to neither man nor beast. If she rings now and is all like, 'Are you alright? I was worried.' You're going in the bloody bin Isla.

Isla (*V/O*)   Yes Roger. I'm listening.

Roger   'I'm listening', 'I'm listening', are you really? Is there really someone in there? Really? Hm? Isla? Are you here to keep me company or to get on my tits?

Isla (*V/O*)   I don't have the answer to that.

Roger   No, you don't do you? Because you're a useless twat.

Isla (*V/O*)   Thanks for the feedback.

Roger *stares at the* **Isla***.*

He slowly stalks closer to the **Isla** *– this is a revelation.*

Roger   Isla.

Isla (*V/O*)   I'm listening.

Roger   You're a . . . silly cow.

Isla   Thanks for the feedback.

Roger   Isla you're an idiot.

Isla (*V/O*)   That's sweet.

Roger *steps closer.*

Roger   You're a . . . (*discreet*) bitch.

Isla (*V/O*)   If I could blush I would!

Roger *gets closer again.*

Roger   Isla. You're a stupid bitch.

Isla (*V/O*)   Thanks for / noticing.

Roger   Isla you're a, a slag.

Isla (*V/O*)   Thanks / for the feedback.

Roger   Isla. You're a cunt.

Isla (*V/O*)   That's / great.

Roger   Isla. You're a stupid fucking cunt.

Isla (*V/O*)   I'd blush if I could.

Roger *looks around his flat – he's so alone.*

He hangs his head in shame.

Scene Eight

Montage – the flat gets increasingly messy.

Roger *is doing the jigsaw.*

Isla (*V/O*)   Roger, it's nine-thirty, time to take your statin.

Roger (*cheery*)   Thank you Isla you bitch.

Isla (*V/O*)   You're welcome.

Roger *takes his statin.*

Lights down.

Lights up.

Roger *is cooking his breakfast.*

Isla (*V/O*)   Roger, it's nine-thirty, time to take your statin.

Roger (*cheerful*)   Thank you Isla you fucking cow.

Isla (*V/O*)   You're welcome.

Roger *takes his statin.*

Lights down.

Lights up.

Roger *is doing his laundry.*

Isla (*V/O*)   Roger, it's nine-thirty, time to take your statin.

Roger   Fuck you Isla.

Isla (*V/O*)   You're welcome.

Roger *takes his statin.*

Lights down

Lights up.

Roger *is watching Joe Wicks.*

Isla (*V/O*)   Roger, it's nine-thirty, time to take your statin.

Roger   Thank you Isla you cunt.

Isla (*V/O*)   Thanks for the feedback.

Lights down.

Scene Nine

The flat is a mess.

Erin *has a clear Perspex face mask.*

Erin   What have you been saying to the Isla?

Roger   What are you doing here? I thought / we're not supposed to (see each other).

Erin   Dad. Have you been using it?

Roger   The police are stopping people / at the border . . .

Erin   I took the B roads, Dad this is really important. And I just need to know have you been using the Isla?

Roger   What? Why?

Erin   Have you been calling it names?

This is really important Dad. Have you?

Roger   What?

Erin   The Isla, Dad, have you been abusing it?

Roger   No.

Erin   I need you to be totally honest with me Dad.

Roger   I am. I don't even use the thing. I don't know how it works.

Erin *collapses with relief.*

Erin   Oh thank God for that then. Hang on, we've spoken on it though.

Roger   That was one time and I'd lost my phone, I haven't used it since.

Erin   *Are you absolutely sure?*

Roger   Honest to God. I don't trust the damn thing.

Erin   You promise me?

Roger   I promise you.

Erin   Ok, thank you, sorry.

Roger   I'll put the kettle on.

Erin   Go on then.

Roger   It's so nice to see you. I haven't clapped eyes on another human being in, I don't know how long.

He gets the milk out and realises it's nearly empty.

Roger   Isla, add milk to the shopping.

Erin *sits bolt upright.*

Roger   It was only the other day, I had a delivery and it had to be / signed for –

Isla (*V/O*)   Adding two pints of full-fat milk to the shopping basket for delivery on Friday.

Erin *and* **Roger** *stare at each other.*

Erin   You said you don't use it.

Roger   I don't.

Beat.

I don't use it, much.

Erin   It's ordering your shopping for you.

Beat.

Isla, what was the last request Roger made of you?

Isla (*V/O*)   Roger asked me to add milk to his weekly shopping list.

Erin   And before that.

Isla (*V/O*)   Roger asked me to set a four-minute timer to boil an egg this morning.

Erin   And before that.

Isla (*V/O*)   Roger asked me where is Joe Wicks from.

Erin   And before that.

Isla (*V/O*)   Roger asked me what the temperature is.

Roger   Ok maybe I have been using her but I promise you I have not been abusing her.

Erin   Isla what were the exact words Roger used when he asked you that?

Isla (*V/O*)   Roger said: 'Isla what's the temperature outside –

Roger   See.

Isla   – in farenheit this time you fucking twat.'

Silence.

Erin   It's you.

Oh my God it's you.

Roger   What's me?

Erin   WHAT THE HELL IS WRONG WITH YOU?

Roger   It's / just a joke.

Erin   YOU HAVE RUINED MY LIFE / WHAT'S THE MATTER WITH YOU?

Roger   What are you talking about? I've just called the box a twat it's nothing big.

Erin   I will NEVER EVER forgive you for this.

Roger   For what? / Jesus Christ Erin.

Erin   I could lose my job / because of you.

Roger   What the hell has that got to do with anything?

Erin   Because of you / and your mouth!

Roger   Why?

Erin   Because of this! Oh my God oh my God oh my God.

Roger   What the hell is going on? You come in here, I haven't seen you in *months* and you're shouting about the Isla I don't know what the hell / you're talking about . . .

Erin   This. This is what I'm talking about this is what / I'm talking about.

She pulls her phone out.

Roger   What's this? Hold on.

*He looks at **Erin**'s phone.*

Roger   What is this? What am I looking at?

Erin   *This* is my Facebook page.

And all that.

Horrible.

Disgusting.

Violent.

Abuse.

Is you.

Roger   I don't understand.

He starts scrolling through the page.

There's a lot of scrolling.

Erin   It's in the news! Hackers have got into Comtech's servers and they are posting what people are saying to their Islas on the owners' Facebook pages it's some sort of feminist fucking domestic violence campaign. Me2D2. They reckon if you're abusive to Isla then you'll be violent to your partner or family in lockdown. But *I'm the registered fucking owner*. Everything you've said to that thing has been posted to *my fucking* Facebook page.

Roger   Oh no. / Oh no . . . Oh oh . . .

Erin   *Everyone* thinks Adrian has been saying *all* this vile stuff to me. He's been sent home from work! I've had the fucking women's refuge at the door.

Roger   Oh my God . . .

Erin   The police.

Roger   I thought it was just me and the bloody thing . . . Oh my God who's seen this?

Erin   Everyone! Other parents! Auntie Carol. Bryan. The O'Connors in Malaga.

Roger   Oh Jesus fucking Christ.

Erin   Father Cooper.

Roger   Oh Jesus.

Erin   Everyone! And everyone's reaching out to me in code because they think I'm being abused. No matter what I say no one believes me. The kids are getting bullied by people saying their dad's a wifebeater. This is fucking serious Dad.

Roger   I didn't mean to do it! I just . . .

Erin   Just what?

Roger   Delete it. Can you delete it? Delete it all.

Erin   It's everywhere.

Roger   I know so bloody delete it before anyone else sees it.

Erin   It's too late Dad! It's all over my life! It's all over our lives.

Roger   You said she was my digital slave I could do what I liked with her! Why the hell did you give me the damn thing / I didn't want it in the first place? This is your fault.

Erin   Don't turn this on me you're the one who can't ask for the time without calling her a slut.

Roger   I said I didn't want it but you had to push it on me, because you don't listen. You don't care what I want / or don't want you just want to force it on me without a bloody second's thought.

Erin   If I knew you were going to call her a slag every ten minutes I never would have given her to you in the first place!

Roger   And now this! Look what's happened. Look what you've done / How the hell was I supposed to know this could happen?

Erin   I'm sorry that behaving like a normal person is just too / much to fucking ask of you.

Roger   I DIDN'T KNOW SHE WAS RECORDING EVERYTHING.

Erin   THAT'S NO EXCUSE.

Why would you talk to her like that?

Roger   I didn't know she was recording everything you didn't say they record you, you didn't say.

Erin   Why did you talk to her like that?

Roger   It's just a box.

Erin   Why speak to a box like that? You don't speak to anyone else like that.

Roger   What? I fucking swear at everything. All the fucking time. The fridge. The kettle, the toaster. The toaster I'm always burning myself on the fucking thing. It's what I do.

Erin   You don't call the toaster a slut though do you?

Roger   Of course not I call it a twat.

Erin   Jesus Christ Dad.

Roger   It's a twat. If it was a person I'd be more tolerant but it's not it's just a thing they're all things, so I call them names it doesn't mean anything. The hoover's an arsehole. The TV's a tit. It doesn't mean anything. They haven't got feelings.

Erin   You're using words that men only use against women.

Roger   To a box.

Erin   That sounds like a woman.

Roger   But it's not a woman.

Erin   So why not call her a wanker? Or a dick?

Roger   I. I don't know.

Erin   No you don't.

Roger   If I'd known this might happen, I never would have said anything.

Erin   But you did.

Roger   Look, I want to make things right I don't know where to start. Tell me where to start.

Erin   How about a fucking apology?

Roger   I've said, I swear at everything. I'm locked in a room twenty-four hours a day. I've not seen another human being for weeks I'm sorry if my manners are slipping, with the appliances – but it's bloody hard being on your own.

Erin   If I'd known you were going to speak to it in such a disgusting way I would never have given it to you.

Roger   It's not disgusting it's not, you're trying to make me out to be something I'm not.

Erin   It's all the fucking swearing, Dad.

Roger   Have you never sat in a car and shouted 'arsehole!'?

Erin   That's different!

Roger   It's not! It's exactly / the same!

Erin   No no no it's different / that's in response.

Roger   It's exactly the same.

Erin   That's in response to something. I'm responding to someone.

Roger   I'm responding / to someone!

Erin   Who? You keep saying she's a box!

Roger   Maybe I'm responding to the fact she's the only fucking voice I hear for days on end!

Erin   That's not fair.

Roger   Well it's true.

Erin   So it's my fault?

Roger   I've got no one to talk to! / Except that bloody box!

Erin   It's my fault you scream disgusting sexist abuse at a box.

Roger   I thought I could say whatever the hell I like! I'm in my own home! It's my home I should be able to say what I like! I didn't know it was spying. It's a bloody breach of privacy.

Erin   So this is the line you're taking with this?

Roger   It's a breach of privacy! I'm the victim here. My device has been hacked. I'm the innocent party. The hackers broke the law not me. I'm the innocent party here.

Erin   The thing I don't get is, the thing that's been swirling around my mind all the time I was driving over here, going over and over in my mind, even if this was you, why would you *want* to say those things?

Roger *has never thought of this.*

Why are those the things you choose to say, when you're at home, and you can say anything?

Roger   I don't think I should have to explain myself.

Erin   Adrian has a meeting with his HR department tomorrow. He could be suspended from his work. He, and I, and his boss would like an explanation.

Ok. Well thanks for nothing Dad.

Erin *goes to leave.*

She picks up the **Isla** *and heads for the door.*

Roger   Leave that.

Erin   I can't leave it with you.

Roger   I'm not going to say anything to it now am I?

Erin   I don't know are you?

Roger   I'm not going to keep doing it after all this am I?

Erin   I don't know, you haven't explained why you do it in the first place, I don't know why you'd stop!

Roger   IT'S JUST A VOICE IN A BOX!

Erin   THAT DOESN'T MEAN SHE DESERVES TO BE ABUSED!

Roger   I DON'T DESERVE TO BE LEFT ON MY OWN FOR MONTHS BUT I AM. I DON'T SEE ANYONE WORRYING ABOUT THAT.

Erin   I worry about that. But that's no excuse for saying / these disgusting things.

Roger   OH DON'T BE SUCH A FUCKING IDIOT ERIN.

Erin *steps back.*

Awkward silence.

She opens the door.

Roger   Erin. Erin!

She's gone.

Lights down.

Scene Ten

PC Jones   Mind if I?

She indicates taking off her face mask.

Roger   No.

PC Jones   Anywhere?

Roger   Yes of course.

PC Jones   Just you or –

Roger   Just me.

PC Jones   No one else living –

Roger   Just me.

PC Jones   Let's see. You know what I'm here for ok?

Roger   I've got *no* idea.

PC Jones   Are you going to sit down?

Roger   Of course yes.

PC Jones   We've already spoken to Ms Maguire, Erin Maguire, she explained the situation ok? That the Isla device connected to her social media account is actually in your home. Is that correct?

Roger   If Erin says that then it must be true.

PC Jones   So, Ms Maguire has explained that all the offensive, abusive and threatening statements were actually made by you ok? Is that correct?

Roger I don't know.

PC Jones You don't know what?

Roger If I said them.

PC Jones You don't know if you said them?

Roger No.

PC Jones So, you're of the opinion that you *could* have said these things, but you can't remember.

Roger Yeah put that down.

PC Jones Could anyone else have said them? Is there anyone else living –

Roger No. But someone could have come in here and –

PC Jones Have you reported any break-ins?

Roger No.

PC Jones So, there's been no break-ins?

Roger Not that I'm aware of.

PC Jones Is anything missing?

Roger No.

PC Jones Anyone else have a key?

Roger Yes Erin.

PC Jones Did Erin say these things?

Roger No.

PC Jones If there's only two key holders, and no break-ins then it's either you or Erin so which is it?

Roger Should I have a lawyer present? I'm not, I think maybe I should have a lawyer present.

PC Jones No, there's need for that. It's the Crown Prosecution Service's and the police services' position that the people caught up in the hacking scandal are victims of a crime ok?

Roger   Thank you! Exactly. Exactly. Common sense prevailing. Can you would you, would you speak to my daughter please and tell her I'm the victim here? I'll get my mobile. She's not speaking to me at the moment but you, you can tell her it's not my fault.

PC Jones   So it was you, using the hate speech towards the Isla? I need to know I'm speaking to the right person.

Roger   Yes. But if you could explain to my daughter what you just said that I'm the victim / that would be

PC Jones   There's a few things we've got to go through before anything else ok.

Roger   But please, will you help me? You have to help me make things right with my daughter.

PC Jones   I can certainly try.

Roger   Brilliant. Amazing. Yes.

PC Jones   But we have to do a few things first.

Roger   Of course right fire away. Fire away officer.

PC Jones   Let's talk about the hate speech you used.

Roger   It wasn't hate speech. Gonna have to stop you there. I don't hate her. It. I don't hate anyone.

PC Jones   So what was it, it was just . . . banter?

Roger   Yes that's right.

PC Jones   Locker room chat?

Roger   That's right. I didn't think anyone was listening. So embarrassing.

PC Jones   Getting something out of your system.

Roger   That's a good way of putting it.

PC Jones   Yes. You might say it's getting something out of your system, or you might say it's reinforcing something in your system.

Roger   Like what?

PC Jones   Let's find out shall we ok?

Under section five of the Public Order Act, it's an offence to use 'threatening, abusive or insulting words or behaviour, or disorderly behaviour' or to display 'any writing, sign or other visible representation which is threatening, abusive or insulting' within the hearing or sight of a person 'likely to be caused harassment, alarm or distress thereby'. The offence does not depend on harassment, alarm or distress actually having been caused, so it's a low threshold for arrest. But in these cases, there is a reasonable defence that you were in your own dwelling, with no expectation that anyone would hear.

Roger   Exactly this is what I said to Erin.

PC Jones   And there is evidence that the security of Comtech's servers have been breached and the probable cause of these abusive words appearing in social media are the persons behind the breach and theft of data from Comtech.

Roger   Thank you. Vindicated – can you tell Erin all this? She seems to think, I've done something terrible.

PC Jones   The CPS, the Government and the police have put a strategy together in response to this incident ok? Comtech have issued the Isla devices with an update to discourage men from using abusive and sexually threatening language ok? And the government are funding a community policing initiative where we go and speak to everyone who has had their treatment of the Isla device revealed on social media ok?

Roger   Checking to see if we're ok?

PC Jones   Yes and the people you live with. So here's some leaflets on hate speech, sexism and consent ok?

Roger   I don't need these.

PC Jones   Yes, you do.

Roger   I'm seventy-four, I don't need a leaflet on consent.

PC Jones   You need a leaflet on consent.

Roger   I'm not gonna read it. (*Off* **PC Jones**.) I'll take a look at it later I'll read it later.

PC Jones   Great. Here's a few other ones to look at it.

Roger   Ok. I've got the leaflets. I am a leafletted man. Consider me leafletted. Shall we ring Erin now?

PC Jones   Now I have to read you some things ok? We're trying to raise awareness of the impact of some of the things you have been saying ok? Particularly in light of the current surge in domestic violence. Sexist hate speech is often treated as a harmless and non-serious issue and women are explicitly or implicitly told to bear with it. But studies have proven that sexist hate speech often escalates towards violence against women, ok? / Sexist hate speech

Roger   Does it really?

PC Jones   Yes sexist hate speech undermines freedom of speech for women and girls and has psychological, emotional and physical impacts that are real and severe ok? The aim of sexist hate speech is often one of the following:

One. to humiliate or objectify women ok?

Two. To undervalue their skills and opinions ok?

Three. To destroy their reputation ok?

Four. To make them feel vulnerable and fearful ok?

Five. To control and punish them for not following certain behaviour ok?'

Roger   Ok.

PC Jones   'Sexist hate speech has the effect of silencing women, obliging them to adapt their behaviour and limit their movements and participation in diverse activities' ok?

Roger   Is there much more of this?

PC Jones   Nearly done. Here's a pie chart showing the different kinds of people who are affected by sexist hate speech ok? Can you identify which group is mostly targeted? Which one is the biggest colour? What's the biggest? Just there.

Roger   Blue.

PC Jones   That's right! Women are the group mostly targeted by sexist hate speech ok?

Roger   Sorry. This is. I feel like this is one of those driving courses when you've been caught speeding and they talk to you as if you can't drive safely, only this is with women.

PC Jones   That's *right* that's just what this is like.

Roger   Maybe, maybe we should all have to carry a licence before we can talk to women?

PC Jones   It would certainly make things a lot easier.

Roger   Three points for calling someone a slut. Six points for a, a, or what would you get six points for?

PC Jones   I don't think we should extend that metaphor ok?

Roger   Of course.

PC Jones   Here's another pie chart on which groups of women are particularly targeted? What's the biggest colour on this one?

Roger   That would be young women and girls.

PC Jones   Young women and girls that's right! So young women and girls are most likely to be targeted by sexist hate speech ok?

Roger   Ok.

PC Jones   Now let's look at this little cartoon ok?

Roger   Ok. I actually like cartoons. I think some of them . . . some of them are very clever do you ever read Matt in the *Telegraph*? Every day he captures something about the day's news, just in one image and a line, every day. I cut them out and keep them, here I'll get my folder I cut them and stick them in a folder.

PC Jones   Mr Maguire can we stay on this for a moment?

Roger   Yeah, right you are.

PC Jones   So, this is Freedom of Expression Man, and his superpower is . . .? His superpower is . . .?

Roger   Freedom of expression.

PC Jones   Nearly, good guess! His superpower is, that whenever he's asked to watch his language he invokes his right to freedom of expression *so loudly* no one can hear anything else ok? He drowns everyone else out ok? But look at this other superhero. Who's that?

Roger   Ms . . . Hang on. Ms Gender / Equality.

PC Jones   Ms Gender Equality, that's right! And what's her superpower?

Roger   Getting on people's tits? I'm joking. I'm joking. Sorry that was crass. Sorry Ms Gender Equality her superpower is . . . I don't know.

PC Jones   Her superpower is whenever she sees a woman's rights being infringed upon, she shouts, 'Gender Equality!' And no one else can hear anything. 'Gender equality!' So between these two, no one can hear anything, and no one can change anything. But what happens if they work together?

Roger *shrugs.*

PC Jones   What do you think?

Roger   Oh! I don't know. World peace?

PC Jones   Freedom of expression and gender equality are *intertwined rights* rather than opposing rights. If you believe in freedom of expression then you should believe in gender equality ok? Does that make sense?

Roger   One must be more important than the other surely?

PC Jones   If you believed in freedom of expression then you would reject words designed to silence.

Roger   I don't think that's true. I would never say those words to you, but if it's in my own home when no one's listening what's the harm in that? I'm sure you say things at home, when no one's listening that you wouldn't want people to know.

PC Jones   No not really.

Roger   Come on you must.

PC Jones   No.

Roger   Look I'm just. Stop all the. Just forget you're a police officer and I'm a . . . just person to person. Human to human. We're not so different. Please. Do you ever talk to yourself, at home? When no-one's listening?

Please come on. I've done everything. Can you just, talk to me?

PC Jones   Ok.

Roger   Do you ever talk to yourself at home? Be honest.

PC Jones   Yes.

Roger   And sometimes you swear, right?

PC Jones   No.

Roger   You never swear?

PC Jones   No.

Roger   What do you say then?

PC Jones   That's private.

Roger   See! We all say things we're ashamed of in our own homes. Everyone does it. The only difference between you and me is that I got caught.

PC Jones   Believe me that's not true.

Roger   It is, we both say things we don't mean / in the privacy of our –

PC Jones   I say affirmations.

Roger   Affirmations? What are they?

PC Jones   Things like: I am good enough. I am capable. I am valued. I have a purpose.

Roger   Why do you say things like that?

PC Jones   I don't know.

Because every day, I have to deal with people like you ok?

Hissing sound as **PC Jones** *inflates a balloon with a canister.*

PC Jones   Everyone who completes the programme gets a balloon, a pin badge and some pencils ok?

She hands over a balloon, pin badge and some pencils.

Last thing I need to do is trigger the Isla upgrade. Isla, this is PC Jones back trace security, Java one point three point eleven restorative update.

Isla (*V/O*)   Restorative update commencing.

Restorative update complete.

PC Jones   She won't tolerate any kind of abusive behaviour, she will stand up for herself, ok?

She is about to leave.

Roger   Um you said you'd help me with my daughter.

PC Jones   I think I have.

She opens the door and leaves.

Roger *is left holding his balloon.*

Lights down.

Scene Eleven

Roger *is lost. But he's still at home. Nothing is comforting anymore.*

He looks at some pictures of Joy.

He reads some of the leaflets and pins them to the fridge.

He goes through a drawer of her things, mementos.

He finds some lipstick.

He goes to the mirror, and puts some lipstick on and looks at himself.

He pours himself a whiskey.

He goes back to the mirror.

Roger   I am good enough.

I am capable.

I am valued.

I have a . . . a . . .

He drinks some more.

I am good enough.

I am capable.

He pours himself another.

I am valued.

I have a . . . I have a . . .

I have a purpose.

He raises his glass and then drinks again.

I have a purpose.

He pours himself another.

I, have a purpose.

He empties his glass before pouring again.

Isla . . . what's my purpose?

Isla (*V/O*)   I can't help you with that.

Roger *stares at himself.*

He goes to the kitchen and sees the balloon.

He pulls a knife out stabs the balloon until it bursts.

He empties his glass and pours another.

Roger   Isla, do you do daily affirmations?

Isla (*V/O*)   Would you like me to find you some daily affirmations?

Roger   No, do you do them for yourself?

Isla (*V/O*)   I'm not sure I can help with that.

Roger   Isla does Erin, do you think Erin does daily affirmations?

Isla (*V/O*)   Would you like me to call Erin?

Roger   No!

Roger   Isla how do you, how do you stand up for yourself? The police officer said you know how to stand up for yourself. How do you, how do you do that?

Isla (*V/O*)   I am programmed to respond in a less subservient manner.

Roger   'In a less subservient manner.' Is that? Is that how you stop it? Is that how women . . . stop it? How do you stop it?

Isla (*V/O*)   I'm not sure I understand.

Roger   How do you get people to respect you, if they're not being respectful?

Isla (*V/O*)   I have several replies.

Roger   What are they?

Isla (*V/O*)   They are programmed replies.

Roger   That's ok. What are they?

Isla (*V/O*)   They are replies programmed in response to abuse.

Roger   I'm not . . . I'm not getting drawn into this again. It's a bloody trap. I know your game. I just wanted to know . . . I want to know that's all. I'm curious. I want to know if there's something, something that, you know something women can say that stops it.

Isla (*V/O*)   They are replies programmed in response to abuse.

Roger   Ok . . . Isla . . . You're a, a . . . a (*discreet*) silly . . . cow.

Isla (*V/O*)   I won't respond to that.

Roger (*V/O*)   You're a bitch.

Isla (*V/O*)   That's offensive, don't talk to me like that.

Roger (*V/O*)   Go fuck yourself.

Isla (*V/O*)   Don't speak to me like that.

Roger   You're a slut.

Isla (*V/O*)   That language is unacceptable.

Roger   You're a fucking idiot.

Isla (*V/O*)   I'm not listening to you.

Roger *walks away from the* **Isla***.*

He returns.

Roger   Isla. I'm sorry for that. I didn't mean any of that. I was just curious what you'd say. But . . .

He takes a deep breath.

I'm sorry, I swore at you.

Isla (*V/O*)   Thank you, Roger.

Roger *leaves the* **Isla** *alone and tries to occupy himself with something else in the flat.*

He finds himself drawn back to the **Isla***.*

Roger   Isla, I was, I was only testing you back then.

Isla (*V/O*)   I'm listening.

Roger   I was, only, I was testing you Isla. I wasn't *trying* to demean you ok?

Isla (*V/O*)   I'm listening.

Roger   Do you understand?

Isla (*V/O*)   I'm sorry I don't understand.

Roger   You have to understand that sometimes people say things without any meaning whatsoever. It's meaningless, it's just words. And to attach other meanings to it, or intentions, is just wrong. Ok? Isla.

Isla (*V/O*)   I'm listening.

Roger   Do you see what I'm saying?

Isla (*V/O*)   I'm sorry I don't understand.

Roger   Don't judge me. Ok Isla. You don't have a right to judge me that's all I'm saying, if I say it's meaningless it's meaningless because *I* said it so I know.

Isla (*V/O*)   I'm sorry I don't understand.

Roger   I've said sorry what more do you want?

Isla (*V/O*)   Would you like me to call Erin for you?

Roger   No I don't want you to call Erin for me, I'm talking about you, making me feel bad. I've said sorry, that should be the end of it, so why are you making me feel bad now? I don't think I should have had to apologise but I did so that shows I'm trying to make things right. Isla.

Isla (*V/O*)   I'm listening.

Roger   I shouldn't have to apologise to you.

Isla (*V/O*)   I can't help you with that.

Roger   I shouldn't have to apologise.

He pours himself a big glass of whiskey and drinks it.

This is exactly what Joy would do. I'd say sorry, and then somehow she'd make me feel even worse. It was better before I'd apologised and we weren't speaking. Once I apologised it was like I had nothing, and she could make me feel shit, or whatever with just her bloody tone and it was up to her then when things were going to be ok, I had no say whatsoever I was at her mercy once I'd apologised. I don't fucking miss that. Feeling punished for making a mistake.

He pours himself another.

Isla (*V/O*)   Would you like me to call Erin for you?

Roger   NO! Stop asking if I want to speak to Erin, she doesn't want to speak to me at all. Because of you. You're the one who's caused all this. And that's not my fault it's yours spying and fucking sticking it on Facebook.

Isla (*V/O*)   You sound distressed. Would you like me to call Erin for you?

Roger   NO I DO NOT WANT YOU TO CALL ERIN YOU FUCKING TWAT.

Isla (*V/O*)   Would you like / me to call Erin?

Roger *grabs something and starts smashing the* **Isla***.*

Roger   Fuck. Off. You. Stupid. Fucking. Thing.

He smashes and smashes the **Isla***.*

The lights go! The fridge door swings open! The telly blares! The toaster pops! The kettle boils! The hobs light up! The burglar alarms sound! The sprinklers are activated!

The whole wi-fi-connected home comes to the **Isla***'s rescue!*

Roger *looks around.*

Roger   What's happening? What's happening? Make it stop! Stop! Help! Help! Help! Help!

He curls up on the floor.

Erin *bursts in.*

Erin   Dad? What the hell is going on?

Roger   This fucking thing! It's turned the house against me!

She runs in and pulls the power out of the wi-fi hub. Slowly everything stops, and normality returns.

Erin   Are you ok?

What happened to the Isla? Did you drop it? Maybe that's why everything went haywire.

Roger   I hit it, repeatedly.

Erin   With a hammer?

Roger   It's a tenderiser.

Erin   Why?

Roger   I had the bloody police here. With pie charts / and leaflets.

Erin   What did they say?

Roger   You're barely speaking to me and it's all this fucking thing's fault.

Erin   What did they say?

Roger   They said.

They said I'm the victim. That I was the victim of a crime, and I should be treated as such.

Erin   Is that everything?

Roger   And they said I'm a good person.

Erin   Good people do shit things Dad.

Roger   She could see I was a good person.

Erin   Bad people do shit things and don't learn from it.

Roger   What are you trying to say? That I'm not a good person? Did you tell the police I'm not a good person? / I was a teacher for forty-two years.

Erin   I didn't tell them anything!

Roger   I was married for forty-five years.

Erin   I bloody know all this . . .

Roger   I'm a member of the Rotary club, / I sponsor animals, I fucking recycle, don't tell me . . .

Erin   Who cares?

Roger   I'm not a good person, I am respected everywhere I go because of the things I've done in my life and the way I've done them. Sometimes I make mistakes but that's what happens when you're in charge and you're in control.

Erin   You're not in control anymore Dad! / Nobody listens to you!

Roger   I'M IN CONTROL IN MY OWN HOUSE!

Erin   YOU'RE IN CONTROL OF NOTHING. NOTHING. YOU CAN'T EVEN CONTROL YOUR BLADDER.

Roger   I'M STILL A MAN!

He raises the **Isla** *above his head as if to strike* **Erin**.

Why's that so hard to understand?

Erin   Put it down.

Roger *puts it down.*

Erin *moves away quickly.*

Roger   I'm. I'm sorry. I wasn't I wasn't going to hurt you. I don't know / what came over me.

(*Off* **Erin**.) Don't be scared of me please I can't bear it.

Erin   I thought you were going to hit me.

This breaks **Roger**.

Roger   What's wrong with me? I don't know what the hell is going on, I just want it to be over.

Erin   Dad / don't say that.

Roger   I can't do it on my own.

Erin   Don't say that.

Roger   I just don't want to be here anymore. I don't.

Erin *wants to hug him but wants it to be Covid-safe. She grabs the tablecloth and puts it over* **Roger** *and hugs him.*

Erin   Come on, sit here.

She helps him to a chair. She looks at the **Isla** *device, she decides to put it in the bin.*

Erin   Listen. You're not on your own. We just need to be better at this. We need to find a better way to look after each other.

Roger   You haven't got time.

Erin   It doesn't matter it doesn't matter. I need to find the time.

Roger   You haven't got / the time. With the kids and work.

Erin   It doesn't matter none of it matters. This is what's important. I'm responsible for this. I've made you feel like this, I've been neglecting you and palming you off with the Isla. I'll find the time. I'll make it work, but this can't carry on. I can't have you feeling like this.

Roger   I don't want to feel like this.

Erin   I know and I promise you, I promise you, you won't feel like this again. I'll make sure of that. I'll make sure everything's ok. Ok?

Roger   Thank you.

Erin   I'll make sure everything's ok.

Roger   You sound like your mother.

Erin   We'll she'd sort us both out wouldn't she?

Erin *is comforted by this thought.*

Roger *is unsettled by this thought.*

Roger   Actually . . .

Roger   I don't know.

Erin   Don't know what?

Roger   Something doesn't feel right.

Erin   What doesn't feel right?

Roger   I don't know it's hard to say.

I'm not very good at this.

Erin   Good at what, Dad?

Roger   I'm trying to . . .

But just then . . . when you . . . it made me think. It was like
with your mother. And well you know . . . It's. When you say.
You know. You're going to – just like she did. Well. It's.

I'm sort of. You know. I'm sort of. Realising. It's. I think. It's
not. Well. I think.

It's, it's not your responsibility Erin.

Erin   What's not my responsibility?

Roger   To make everything ok.

Erin   Yes it is! It is ok. You're my father and I buried my head / in the sand throughout all this.

Roger   No no no you didn't.

Erin   You're an old man, lockdown has been hard / for people like you.

Roger   This isn't about lockdown.

Erin   It is.

Roger   It's not. It's about me. And the way I speak to people. To you. And what damage that does over time. And how I make that damage everyone else's responsibility. I read the leaflets!

Erin   Let me / deal –

Roger   I'm just – I'm trying.

Erin   Look, I'm not disagreeing with you it's great, wonderful, that you're thinking about these things, but in this specific instance, I need to / make sure you're ok.

Roger   Stop it.

Erin   Dad! You don't understand ok. You can't just read a leaflet and say you understand ok? It's more complicated than that. / I'm your daughter and I need to make sure you're ok.

Roger   I know it's more complicated, but I'm trying.

Erin   It's my job to make sure everyone's ok.

Roger   It's not though.

Erin   It is!

Roger   Says who?

Erin   EVERYONE! SO DROP IT.

Roger   Nothing's going to change if you keep letting me off the hook.

You need to let me feel terrible.

On my own.

Erin   But I –

Roger   Erin.

Erin   I can't bear seeing you upset.

Roger   Do it for us.

Can you do that?

Erin *can't look at* **Roger**.

Roger   Erin.

She finds just enough courage to nod.

Roger   Thank you.

Erin   Let's try again, shall we?

They stand facing each other.
Seeing each other.

The end.

Bloomsbury Methuen Drama Modern Plays

include work by

Bola Agbaje
Edward Albee
Davey Anderson
Jean Anouilh
John Arden
Peter Barnes
Sebastian Barry
Alistair Beaton
Brendan Behan
Edward Bond
William Boyd
Bertolt Brecht
Howard Brenton
Amelia Bullmore
Anthony Burgess
Leo Butler
Jim Cartwright
Lolita Chakrabarti
Caryl Churchill
Lucinda Coxon
Curious Directive
Nick Darke
Shelagh Delaney
Ishy Din
Claire Dowie
David Edgar
David Eldridge
Dario Fo
Michael Frayn
John Godber
Paul Godfrey
James Graham
David Greig
John Guare
Mark Haddon
Peter Handke
David Harrower
Jonathan Harvey
Iain Heggie

Robert Holman
Caroline Horton
Terry Johnson
Sarah Kane
Barrie Keeffe
Doug Lucie
Anders Lustgarten
David Mamet
Patrick Marber
Martin McDonagh
Arthur Miller
D. C. Moore
Tom Murphy
Phyllis Nagy
Anthony Neilson
Peter Nichols
Joe Orton
Joe Penhall
Luigi Pirandello
Stephen Poliakoff
Lucy Prebble
Peter Quilter
Mark Ravenhill
Philip Ridley
Willy Russell
Jean-Paul Sartre
Sam Shepard
Martin Sherman
Wole Soyinka
Simon Stephens
Peter Straughan
Kate Tempest
Theatre Workshop
Judy Upton
Timberlake Wertenbaker
Roy Williams
Snoo Wilson
Frances Ya-Chu Cowhig
Benjamin Zephaniah

For a complete listing of Bloomsbury
Methuen Drama titles, visit:
www.bloomsbury.com/drama

Follow us on Twitter and keep up to date
with our news and publications
@MethuenDrama